US MILITARY

GREEN BERETS

BY JESSICA COUPÉ

WWW.APEXEDITIONS.COM

Copyright © 2023 by Apex Editions, Mendota Heights, MN 55120. All rights reserved. No part of this book may be reproduced or utilized in any form or by any means without written permission from the publisher.

Apex is distributed by North Star Editions:
sales@northstareditions.com | 888-417-0195

Produced for Apex by Red Line Editorial.

Photographs ©: Shutterstock Images, cover, 1, 4–5, 7, 8–9, 9, 12–13, 16–17, 18, 22–23, 24–25, 26, 26–27, 29; AP Images, 10–11; iStockphoto, 14–15, 19; Ken Kassens/U.S. Army/AP Images, 21

Library of Congress Control Number: 2022901415

ISBN
978-1-63738-308-7 (hardcover)
978-1-63738-344-5 (paperback)
978-1-63738-412-1 (ebook pdf)
978-1-63738-380-3 (hosted ebook)

Printed in the United States of America
Mankato, MN
082022

NOTE TO PARENTS AND EDUCATORS

Apex books are designed to build literacy skills in striving readers. Exciting, high-interest content attracts and holds readers' attention. The text is carefully leveled to allow students to achieve success quickly. Additional features, such as bolded glossary words for difficult terms, help build comprehension.

TABLE OF CONTENTS

CHAPTER 1
ON A MISSION 4

CHAPTER 2
HISTORY 10

CHAPTER 3
TRAINING 16

CHAPTER 4
GREEN BERETS TODAY 22

COMPREHENSION QUESTIONS • 28
GLOSSARY • 30
TO LEARN MORE • 31
ABOUT THE AUTHOR • 31
INDEX • 32

CHAPTER 1

ON A MISSION

A team of Green Berets sneak into enemy territory. The soldiers wear night-vision goggles to see in the dark. They spot someone coming toward them.

Green Berets soldiers must be ready to fight day or night.

FAST FACT
Green Berets soldiers can speak at least two languages.

The Green Berets are ready to shoot. But the man speaks. He says he is a **resistance** leader. He wants to free his country from unfair rulers.

The Green Berets travel to many countries for their missions.

WHY THE NAME?

Green Berets belong to the US Army Special Forces. Their name comes from the hats they wear. The hats help people tell Green Berets apart from other Army soldiers.

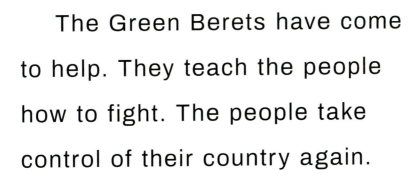

The Green Berets have come to help. They teach the people how to fight. The people take control of their country again.

◀ Green Berets and other US Army Special Forces do missions that are extra dangerous.

CHAPTER 2

History

The Green Berets were formed in 1952. They were based on other groups of fighters. These groups did special work for the US Army.

A group of Green Berets prepare for a mission in 1962.

For some missions, Green Berets hide in swamps.

The Green Berets use **guerilla** fighting. They hide and wait for the enemy. Then they jump out and attack.

FAST FACT

The Green Berets have a motto. It says, "To Free the **Oppressed**."

In 2001, Green Berets went to Afghanistan to help resistance fighters.

14

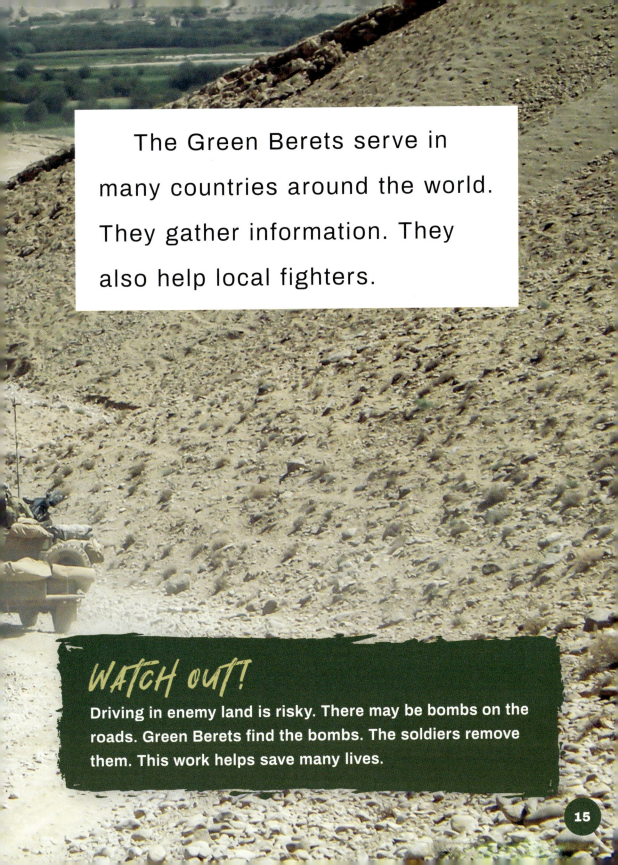

The Green Berets serve in many countries around the world. They gather information. They also help local fighters.

WATCH OUT!

Driving in enemy land is risky. There may be bombs on the roads. Green Berets find the bombs. The soldiers remove them. This work helps save many lives.

CHAPTER 3

TRAINING

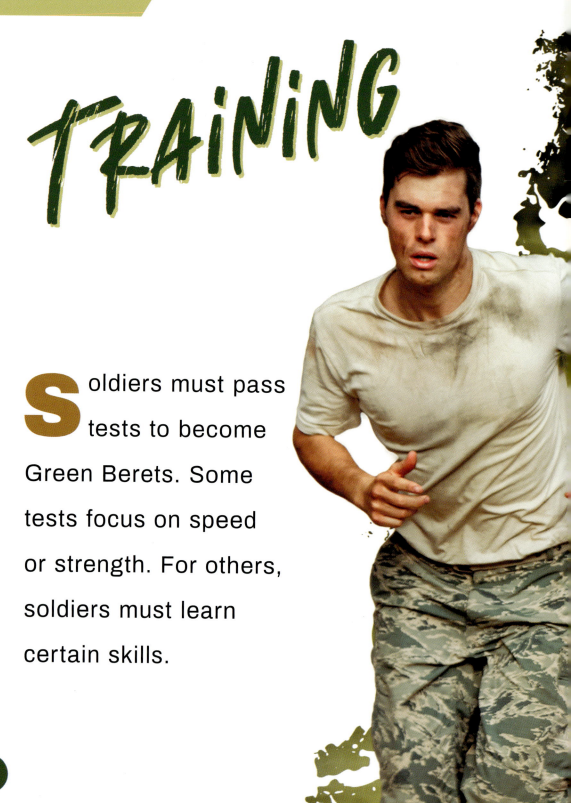

Soldiers must pass tests to become Green Berets. Some tests focus on speed or strength. For others, soldiers must learn certain skills.

Green Berets must be able to run 2 miles (3 km) in less than 14 minutes.

Green Berets learn to use many weapons. They train others to use weapons, too.

FAST FACT

Green Berets can do 100 push-ups in two minutes.

Making a fire is one important survival skill that soldiers learn.

For example, soldiers learn how to survive in the **wilderness**. They also study other **cultures**. This training prepares them for missions in other countries.

HALO JUMPS

Green Berets practice HALO jumps. A plane flies high above the ground. Soldiers leap out. They don't open their parachutes until they're close to the ground. This helps them stay hidden.

The last test is a practice mission. It lasts a few weeks. The soldiers fight in a fake war. They practice the skills they have learned. If they pass, they become Green Berets.

The final test for Green Berets takes place in the North Carolina woods.

CHAPTER 4

GREEN BERETS TODAY

Today, Green Berets work in more than 80 countries. They are known as the "quiet **professionals**." That's because they often work in secret.

Green Berets may wear camouflaged clothing. Its colors help them hide during missions.

Green Berets do many kinds of missions. They might wreck enemy equipment. Or they might find out enemy plans. That way, they can help stop attacks.

On a Green Beret team, a spotter (right) finds the target. A sniper (left) shoots the target.

TEAMWORK

Green Berets work in teams. Every team has 12 members. Each person has different skills. Some know about weapons. Others do first aid. Together, they use their skills to complete missions.

Green Berets may train fighters in **foreign** countries. By helping these other countries, Green Berets also help protect the United States.

Green Berets may use parachutes to reach some countries.

Green Berets are some of the deadliest fighters in the world.

FAST FACT
For some missions, Green Berets rescue people who have been captured.

COMPREHENSION QUESTIONS

Write your answers on a separate piece of paper.

1. Write a sentence that explains the main ideas of Chapter 2.

2. Would you like to wear night-vision goggles? Why or why not?

3. What is the last test soldiers must pass to become Green Berets?
    - A. a strength test
    - B. a HALO jump
    - C. a practice mission

4. How would finding out enemy plans help Green Berets stop attacks?
    - A. They can act before enemies do.
    - B. They can warn the enemies.
    - C. They can join the enemies.

5. What does **rescue** mean in this book?

For some missions, Green Berets rescue people who have been captured.

  A. run
  B. save
  C. lose

6. What does **risky** mean in this book?

Driving in enemy land is risky. There may be bombs on the roads.

  A. full of danger
  B. full of peace
  C. not possible

Answer key on page 32.

GLOSSARY

cultures
Groups of people and the ways they live, including their beliefs and laws.

foreign
Being in a country or using a language other than your own.

guerilla
A style of fighting that uses surprise attacks.

oppressed
People who are treated in a cruel or unfair way.

parachutes
Fabrics that open up to slow people's falls through the air.

professionals
People who get paid to do a job.

resistance
A group of people who fight against their country's leaders or against an invading army.

wilderness
A place without people.

TO LEARN MORE

BOOKS

Bassier, Emma. *Military Gear*. Minneapolis: Abdo Publishing, 2020.

Gish, Melissa. *Green Berets*. Mankato, MN: Creative Paperbacks, 2021.

Head, Tom. *Green Berets*. Mankato, MN: Black Rabbit Books, 2019.

ONLINE RESOURCES

Visit www.apexeditions.com to find links and resources related to this title.

ABOUT THE AUTHOR

Jessica Coupé is the author of several children's books. When not writing, she is learning about her ancestors' stories. She lives in British Columbia, Canada.

INDEX

A
attacks, 12, 24

C
countries, 6, 9, 15, 19, 22, 26

E
enemy, 4, 12, 15, 24

F
fighters, 10, 15, 26
formed, 10

G
guerilla, 12

M
missions, 19–20, 24, 25, 27

N
night-vision goggles, 4

S
secret, 22
skills, 16, 20, 25
soldiers, 4, 6, 9, 16, 19–20

T
teams, 4, 25
tests, 16, 20
training, 19, 26

U
US Army, 9, 10

W
weapons, 25

ANSWER KEY:
1. Answers will vary; 2. Answers will vary; 3. C; 4. A; 5. B; 6. A